GREAT
AMERICAN PRESIDENTS

FRANKLIN DELANO
ROOSEVELT

GREAT AMERICAN PRESIDENTS

John Adams

John Quincy Adams

Jimmy Carter

Thomas Jefferson

John F. Kennedy

Abraham Lincoln

Ronald Reagan

Franklin Delano Roosevelt

Theodore Roosevelt

Harry S. Truman

George Washington

Woodrow Wilson

———— GREAT ————
AMERICAN PRESIDENTS

FRANKLIN DELANO
ROOSEVELT

ALAN ALLPORT

FOREWORD BY
WALTER CRONKITE

CHELSEA HOUSE
PUBLISHERS
A Haights Cross Communications Company

Philadelphia

CHELSEA HOUSE PUBLISHERS

VP, NEW PRODUCT DEVELOPMENT Sally Cheney
DIRECTOR OF PRODUCTION Kim Shinners
CREATIVE MANAGER Takeshi Takahashi
MANUFACTURING MANAGER Diann Grasse

STAFF FOR FRANKLIN DELANO ROOSEVELT

ASSISTANT EDITOR Kate Sullivan
PRODUCTION ASSISTANT Megan Emery
ASSISTANT PHOTO EDITOR Noelle Nardone
SERIES DESIGNER Keith Trego
COVER DESIGNER Keith Trego
LAYOUT 21st Century Publishing and Communications, Inc.

A Haights Cross Communications Company

www.chelseahouse.com

First Printing

1 3 5 7 9 8 6 4 2

Library of Congress Cataloging-in-Publication Data

Allport, Alan.
    Franklin Delano Roosevelt/by Alan Allport.
        p. cm.—(Great American presidents)
Summary: A biography of the thirty-second president whose three terms in office
spanned the years of the Depression and the Second World War. Includes bibliographical
references and index.
    ISBN 0-7910-7598-2 (hardcover)
    1. Roosevelt, Franklin D. (Franklin Delano), 1882-1945—Juvenile literature.
2. Presidents—United States—Biography—Juvenile literature. [1. Roosevelt,
Franklin D. (Franklin Delano), 1882-1945. 2. Presidents.] I. Title. II. Series.
E807.A7825 2003
973.917'092—dc21
                                                                          2003009493

TABLE OF CONTENTS

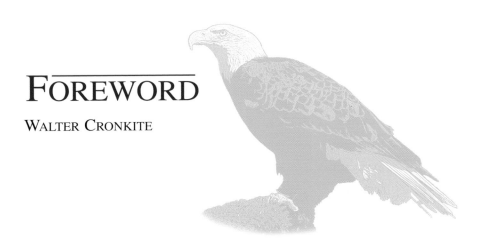

FOREWORD

WALTER CRONKITE

A candle can defy the darkness. It need not have the power of a great searchlight to be a welcome break from the gloom of night. So it goes in the assessment of leadership. He who lights the candle may not have the skill or imagination to turn the light that flickers for a moment into a perpetual glow, but history will assign credit to the degree it is due.

Some of our great American presidents may have had a single moment that bridged the chasm between the ordinary and the exceptional. Others may have assured their lofty place in our history through the sum total of their accomplishments.

When asked who were our greatest presidents, we cannot fail to open our list with the Founding Fathers who put together this nation and nursed it through the difficult years of its infancy. George Washington, John Adams, Thomas Jefferson, and James Madison took the high principles of the revolution against British tyranny and turned the concept of democracy into a nation that became the beacon of hope to oppressed peoples around the globe.

Almost invariably we add to that list our wartime presidents—Abraham Lincoln, perhaps Woodrow Wilson, and certainly Franklin Delano Roosevelt.

Nonetheless there is a thread of irony that runs through the inclusion of the names of those wartime presidents: In many aspects their leadership was enhanced by the fact that, without objection from the people, they assumed extraordinary powers to pursue victory over the nation's enemies (or, in the case of Lincoln, the Southern states).

The complexities of the democratic procedures by which the United States Constitution deliberately tried to withhold unchecked power from the presidency encumbered the presidents who needed their hands freed of the entangling bureaucracy that is the federal government.

Much of our history is written far after the events themselves took place. History may be amended by a much later generation seeking a precedent to justify an action considered necessary at the latter time. The history, in a sense, becomes what later generations interpret it to be.

President Jefferson in 1803 negotiated the purchase of vast lands in the south and west of North America from the French. The deal became knows as the Louisiana Purchase. A century and a half later, to justify seizing the nation's steel mills that were being shut down by a labor strike, President Truman cited the Louisiana Purchase as a case when the president in a major matter ignored Congress and acted almost solely on his own authority.

The case went to the Supreme Court, which overturned Truman six to three. The chief justice, Fred Vinson, was one of the three justices who supported the president. Many historians, however, agreed with the court's majority, pointing out that Jefferson scarcely acted alone: Members of Congress were in the forefront of the agitation to consummate the Louisiana Purchase and Congress voted to fund it.

With more than two centuries of history and precedent now behind us, the Constitution is still found to be flexible when honest and sincere individuals support their own causes with quite different readings of it. These are the questions that end up for interpretation by the Supreme Court.

As late as the early years of the twenty-first century, perhaps the most fateful decision any president ever can make—to commit the nation to war—was again debated and precedent ignored. The Constitution says that only the Congress has the authority to declare war. Yet the Congress, with the objection of few members, ignored this Constitutional provision and voted to give President George W. Bush the right to take the United States to war whenever and under whatever conditions he decided.

Thus a president's place in history may well be determined by how much power he seizes or is granted in re-interpreting and circumventing the remarkable document that is the Constitution. Although the Founding Fathers thought they had spelled out the president's authority in their clear division of powers between the branches of the executive, the legislative and the judiciary, their wisdom has been challenged frequently by ensuing generations. The need and the demand for change is dictated by the march of events, the vast alterations in society, the global condition beyond our influence, and the progress of technology far beyond the imaginations of any of the generations which preceded them.

The extent to which the powers of the presidency will be enhanced and utilized by the chief executives to come in large degree will depend, as they have throughout our history, on the character of the presidents themselves. The limitations on those powers, in turn, will depend on the strength and will of those other two legs of the three-legged stool of American government—the legislative and the judiciary.

And as long as this nation remains a democracy, the final say will rest with an educated electorate in perpetual exercise of its constitutional rights to free speech and a free and alert press.

1

TIMES OF CRISIS

DURING ITS HISTORY, the United States experienced four great crises. The first was the revolution against Great Britain, led by the American colonies' first general and statesman, George Washington. The second was the Civil War of 1861–1865, in which President Abraham Lincoln successfully fought secession and abolished the evil of slavery. The other two occurred less than ten years apart during the twentieth century. One was an economic crisis beginning in 1929, a devastating collapse of the country's business and financial system known as the Great Depression. The other crisis—World War II—reached American shores on the morning of December 7, 1941, when Japanese

Although the devastating effects of polio forced FDR to use a wheelchair after age 39, he was careful never to be photographed in it. His desire and perseverance to pursue his political career helped him secure the Democratic nomination and eventually the presidency—a feat he may not have been able to accomplish had the public perceived him as disabled.

planes attacked the U.S. Pacific Fleet in Hawaii. This war, the largest and most dreadful in human history, pitted the American nation and its allies against dictatorships across the world in a desperate battle for survival. During both of these terrible ordeals, America was led by one man: Franklin Delano Roosevelt, the 32nd and longest-serving president of the United States.

Roosevelt—known to millions simply by his initials, FDR—was a mixture of opposites. He was born into a highly privileged life of wealth and opportunity, but he became the champion of the American poor and dispossessed. He was in many ways a conservative thinker, without any grand plans or ideas, but he revolutionized the role of government and turned America into a great world power. He founded his reputation on simple, catchy phrases—"the New Deal" and "the Four Freedoms"—but he was also a masterful, sometimes even devious, politician. He cultivated a style of friendliness and optimism, but he was hated by his many opponents. Strangest of all, he was one of the most active presidents in American history, traveling farther and doing more than any predecessor in the White House, yet he was a man who was almost paralyzed below the waist because of the devastating illness polio.

Roosevelt's presidency, like those of Washington and Lincoln before him, was a defining moment in

> "We look forward to a world founded upon four essential human freedoms. The first is freedom of speech and expression—everywhere in the world. The second is freedom of everyone to worship God in his own way, everywhere in the world. The third is freedom from want . . . everywhere in the world. The fourth is freedom from fear . . . anywhere in the world."
>
> —FDR, speech, January 6, 1941

the story of the United States. Just as the eighteenth-century revolution brought the nation into being and the nineteenth-century civil war gave it renewed strength and justice, the depression and world war of FDR's era also transformed America. Many of the most pressing questions of the twenty-first century—should the United States play the role of global superpower? should Americans reduce "Big Government" in Washington?—are direct legacies of the Roosevelt years. To understand them better, it is necessary to return to the life and work of the man who some claim is the most important American citizen of the twentieth century.

2

EARLY DAYS:
1882–1910

FRANKLIN DELANO ROOSEVELT was born on January 30, 1882 at his family's home, known as "Springwood," in Hyde Park, New York. Hyde Park is about eight miles north of the city of Pough-keepsie in the beautiful Hudson River Valley. The Springwood estate, which was to figure so prominently in the future president's life, had originally been built as a simple farmhouse around 1826. In 1867, Franklin's father James Roosevelt bought it for $40,000, and for the next 33 years James spent much time and money enlarging the house, adding new servant's quarters, guest rooms, and a carriage house for horses and wagons. By the time Franklin was born, Springwood had become a large and impressive family

Franklin Delano Roosevelt was born on January 30, 1882, in Hyde Park, New York. A member of the wealthy and prominent Roosevelt family, Franklin would nevertheless grow up with a sense of duty and strong desire to perform public service.

mansion, surrounded by lush fields and woodlands. It is little wonder that he grew to love the place so much, and devoted so much energy to its upkeep. The Roosevelt family motto was "Qui plantavit curabit," a Latin phrase that translates "The one who planted it will take care of it"; Franklin took his responsibility as caretaker of his family's home very seriously.

The Roosevelts were an illustrious New York dynasty. The first Roosevelts to reach America were Dutch settlers who had emigrated from the Netherlands to New York (which was then known as "New Amsterdam") in the 1640s. The family had become rich through trade, banking, and real estate, and by the late nineteenth century its members played an important role in the social and political life of New York State. They had also married well, forging alliances with New York's other wealthy and powerful families. Franklin's closest and most illustrious relative was his fifth cousin, Theodore (or "Teddy") Roosevelt, who served as the 26th president of the United States from 1901 to 1909 and was to be a powerful influence on the young man. But Franklin, who was always keen on researching his family tree, could also claim kinship to at least ten other United States presidents, as well as the Confederate general Robert E. Lee and the Confederate president Jefferson Davis. Although Franklin was born into a family network of money and privilege, he had a strong sense of public duty, a commitment that was likely rooted in the Roosevelt family belief that they had not only a right but also a responsibility to help govern America.

> "[The Roosevelts] never felt that because they were born in a good position they could put their hands in their pockets and succeed."
> —From Roosevelt's sophomore honors thesis at Harvard

Franklin's father, James, was well into his sixties by the time his son was born and had lived a prosperous and busy life as a well-traveled lawyer and businessman. James's first wife, Rebecca, bore his first son (also called James) and died in 1876; four years after Rebecca's death,

James Roosevelt married again, this time to a much younger sixth cousin, Sara Delano—Franklin's mother. Sara came from a well-known New York family of commercial traders and had lived an exotic early life in China and Europe. Sara was devoted to her husband, whom she loved dearly, and after Franklin was born in 1882, she was devoted to her infant son as well. Franklin was James and Sara's only child together.

The boy's early years at Springwood were idyllic. With his half-brother James already a grown man by the 1880s, Franklin was pampered and spoiled by his doting parents, having all their attention to himself. His parents tended to keep Franklin in dresses and grow his hair in long curls, which was not unusual for young boys in rich Victorian families, and he also wore kilts and sailor suits. The family often traveled on vacation, either to Europe or to fashionable resorts on the New England shore, as well as to New Brunswick's Campobello Island, where Franklin developed a life-long passion for sailing.

He was educated entirely at home by governesses and private tutors until age 14, when his parents decided to send him to Groton Preparatory School in Massachusetts, about 35 miles northwest of Boston. Groton was a famous private boarding school for young gentlemen in grades 8 through 12, with a roster of distinguished older boys. Franklin was not a particularly brilliant student while at Groton, preferring sports, drama, and the debating club to academic work. At first he found it difficult to fit in among boys his own age, having been relatively isolated

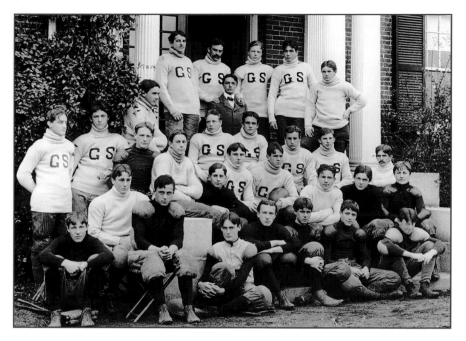

Franklin, the second boy seated on the left, poses for this photograph of the Groton Preparatory School's football team. At age 14, Roosevelt left his private tutors and his home schooling to be educated in the more formalized surroundings of Groton. This experience would serve as a foundation to prepare him for Harvard University.

from other children at Springwood. But in time he became well liked by his fellow students and teachers. At Franklin's graduation, his headmaster, Endicott Peabody, described the young Roosevelt as "a thoroughly faithful scholar and a most satisfactory member of this school throughout his course" with whom he "part[ed] with reluctance." A boy with Franklin's sort of elite social background had little difficulty in gaining acceptance to Harvard College in 1900, despite his less-than-stellar academic performance at school: At the turn of the twentieth century, entrance into an Ivy League college depended more on the right family connections than examination scores. As at Groton, Franklin's performance as an undergraduate was acceptable, but not particularly impressive. He became editor of Harvard's undergraduate newspaper, *The Crimson,* and joined a number of social clubs and societies. But the most prestigious student group of all, Porcellian, to which his father had belonged, rejected him. Franklin felt the bitterness of this unexplained snub for many years afterward.

Several events that took place during Franklin's time at Harvard were to have a profound influence on the rest of his life. During Franklin's first freshman semester, his father, who had been ailing for some time, died. Then, the following year, Franklin's cousin Teddy Roosevelt became president of the United States after the assassination of President William McKinley. Since his days at Groton, Teddy had been an important confidant and role model to Franklin, so much so that the young man even began to wear a pair of the small pince-nez spectacles made fashionable by the elder Roosevelt. Teddy, who had been governor of New York and vice president of the United States, as well as having served with military distinction in the Spanish-American War of 1898, was already an impressive figure. However, his sudden accession to the highest office in the United States made him even more illustrious in Franklin's eyes. Thoughts of following his cousin into a career in public office began to stir in the young undergraduate's mind.

But the most important person in Franklin's life at Harvard was his fifth cousin, Anna Eleanor Roosevelt. Eleanor, who was also Teddy Roosevelt's niece, had not had nearly as happy a childhood as Franklin. Although born into wealth like Franklin, Eleanor's parents were distant, self-absorbed, and insensitive. Her mother, a society beauty, made no secret of her disappointment with Eleanor, and her father, though charming and generous, was an alcoholic with unstable mood swings and fits of depression. Both parents died before Eleanor reached her teens. Having spent the rest of her childhood with an unloving grandmother, she became insular and convinced of her plain looks and dull wits. Franklin, however, saw that Eleanor was an attractive and smart girl who needed only to be released from her own insecurity. She was also deeply committed to issues of social welfare and justice, themes that would become important during her later public career: On several occasions during their courtship Franklin accompanied Eleanor to dilapidated New York City tenements where she did voluntary aid work, introducing the privileged young man to a world of poverty he had never seen before. Franklin was entranced by his cousin. He proposed marriage, and the astonished and flattered Eleanor accepted.

Franklin's mother was unhappy with the match. Not only did she think the couple too young for wedlock—Franklin was 21 and Eleanor just 19—but she was afraid that a new wife would come between her and her beloved only child. Eleanor wrote to her prospective mother-in-law

Anna Eleanor Roosevelt was a distant cousin to Franklin. While Franklin was attending Harvard, he became impressed by her commitment to social justice and fell in love with her. The young couple married on March 17, 1905.

to try to ease the tensions: "I know just how you feel and how hard it must be, but I do so want you to learn to love me a little . . . it is impossible for me to tell you how I feel towards Franklin, [*sic*] I can only say that my one great wish is to prove worthy of him." Sara was unmoved.

Despite his mother's attempts to delay the wedding, however, Franklin was equally stubborn, so on March 17, 1905, the young pair were finally married, with Teddy Roosevelt giving away the bride. As the president's niece, Eleanor was much better known at this time than Franklin, and she was the focus of all the public attention: Franklin later joked that he had been continually congratulated for getting his new wife, but that no one had congratulated Eleanor on getting him! The two Roosevelts settled down into comfortable domestic life in New York City, and their first child, Anna, was born a year after the wedding. Franklin and Eleanor would have four more children—James (1907), Elliott (1910), Franklin Junior (1914), and John (1916)—with another boy dying in infancy.

Since leaving Harvard and marrying Eleanor, Franklin had not given his career much thought. Money was not a pressing issue, given his family's wealth, and Franklin became a law student—not from any deep-seated interest in becoming an attorney, but because his late father had always wanted him to study it. In 1907, Franklin passed the New York bar examination and joined a Manhattan legal firm specializing in business contracts. The work bored him desperately. He yearned to do something more interesting. The old boyhood idea of following in Teddy's political footsteps nagged at him. One day, while idly discussing plans for the future with other law clerks, Franklin suddenly announced

> *"It is common sense to take a method and try it; if it fails, admit it frankly and try another. But above all, try something."*
> —Roosevelt, speech, May 23, 1932

that he would become president of the United States. First, though, he would become state governor like his cousin: "Anyone who is Governor of New York has a good chance to be President with any luck." Franklin's colleagues could not decide if they were more astonished by his audacity or by the self-assured confidence with which he spoke.

Franklin did not have long to wait before he could begin his ascent to power. In 1910, New York State elections were scheduled in Dutchess County, which included Hyde Park and Springwood. The local Democratic Party decided to ask Franklin to contest the state senate seat. Already tired of his dull law career, he eagerly accepted the nomination. It was an uphill struggle. Only a single Democratic nominee had won that particular senate seat since the Civil War. But Franklin threw himself into the campaign with unprecedented gusto, making up for his inexperience with his raw enthusiasm and conviction. He toured Dutchess County in a motorcar, the first political candidate ever to do so, attracting plenty of attention wherever he went—cars were still novelties for most Americans before the First World War. Franklin had other advantages too: a famous surname, plenty of private campaign funds, and a weakened Republican opposition distracted by ruinous internal fighting. The result on Election Day was a 52 percent vote for Franklin over the incumbent senator. The hesitant youngster had found his place in life at last. For the next 35 years, despite many serious setbacks and defeats, Franklin would never lose his essential passion for the world of politics.

3

COURAGE
THROUGH
ADVERSITY:
1911–1932

IT MIGHT SEEM strange at first glance that Franklin D. Roosevelt became a Democrat. After all, his famous cousin and role model was a former Republican president. But Teddy Roosevelt had always been something of a maverick in his own party anyway, and in 1912 he ran as the independent Bull Moose candidate against Republican President Taft, a man he had personally installed in the White House just four years earlier. What mattered more than party labels was that both Teddy and Franklin considered themselves Progressives. The Progressives at the beginning of the twentieth century were eager to weed out dishonesty and corruption in American politics and society, and extend the helping hand of government to ordinary people. Franklin was never a systematic political thinker, and he did not take with him into office a detailed philosophy of his ideas, nor did he develop one during the 20-year apprenticeship that he spent in preparing for his role as president. But he always stayed true to the basic Progressive belief that the government should be a friend to the working man and woman, and prevent the rich and powerful from corrupting the American republic.

The new representative in New York's capital, Albany, soon found himself a worthy enemy to battle. At the time of Roosevelt's election, state politics in New York were almost entirely controlled by a clique of Democratic Party bosses known collectively as "Tammany Hall," after the name of the group's Manhattan headquarters. The Tammany bosses routinely rigged elections, swindled public money from government contracts, and intimidated their opponents. Roosevelt, as an independently wealthy upstate senator, did not rely on Tammany patronage and was free to take the fraudulent bosses on. He led a campaign to stop the nomination of a Tammany favorite, William Sheehan, to the U.S. Senate, for in those days federal senators were still appointed by their state legislatures rather than voted into office by direct election. The Tammany bosses finally replaced Sheehan with a candidate who was even more loyal to them, but nonetheless Roosevelt and his supporters had won a partial victory against

Tammany Hall, the building in the middle, was the headquarters of New York City's Democratic Party. It was home to a notorious group of corrupt politicians whom Roosevelt fought to keep out of public office.

strong institutional corruption. More important, he had also received national media attention for his stand against Tammany—a priceless commodity for an ambitious young politician.

Roosevelt had other pioneering causes as well. He supported extending voting rights to women—a controversial topic at the time—and new laws limiting the maximum number of days in a work week, as well as a national compensation program for sick and unemployed workers. He also took a strong interest in environmental conservation, a theme that was to recur throughout his career. In one speech to state electors, he argued in favor of new laws banning the wanton destruction of New York's forests. "It is necessary for our health and happiness of the whole people of the state," he said, "that individuals and lumber companies should not go into our wooded areas like the Adirondacks and the Catskills and cut them off root and branch for the benefit of their own pocket."

> *"I am a Christian and a Democrat—that's all."*
>
> —Roosevelt, quoted in *The Roosevelt I Knew* by Frances Perkins, Roosevelt's secretary of labor

In 1912, Roosevelt easily gained reelection to the state senate. The same year, however, the Democratic Party candidate Woodrow Wilson won the U.S. presidency, and this opened up an opportunity for Franklin to enter the federal government. The job he most desired was that of assistant secretary of the U.S. Navy, because it was the same post that his cousin Teddy had held during his rise to power 15 years earlier. The Wilson administration was aware of this and was eager to take onboard the effective and well-known young statesman. Roosevelt threw himself into his new role at the navy, pushing for more spending on the fleet and an active foreign policy abroad. This intensified when war broke out in Europe in August 1914, and Franklin—who believed that the United States should intervene in the conflict on the Allied side—found himself at odds with his more cautious and pacific boss, navy secretary Josephus Daniels. The headstrong Roosevelt did not always behave appropriately toward his older superior. The same year that war broke out, however, Franklin received an embarrassing defeat when his attempt to win one of New York's U.S. Senate seats was crushed by resentful Tammany Hall bosses. The failure was a wake-up call: Even a Roosevelt could not afford to make too many enemies. For the rest of his political career, Franklin always worked hard to build strategic alliances with other politicians who could be useful to him, even when he did not care for their ideas.

When the United States finally entered the European war (now known as World War I) in April 1917, Roosevelt attempted to resign his government post and gain an army commission, hoping to recreate his cousin Teddy's battlefield exploits from the Spanish-American conflict. But President Wilson made it clear that he could not spare his assistant navy secretary, so Franklin had to be content with an official trip to France in 1918 where he was able to take a close look at the fighting line. However, on his return to the United States, a crisis in his private life overcame Roosevelt's military ambitions. First he caught pneumonia and was very ill for some weeks. Then Eleanor

Roosevelt, far left, stands a step apart from the other navy officials in this 1915 photograph. President Woodrow Wilson appointed Roosevelt assistant secretary of the navy, affording him the opportunity to serve in the country's military and follow in his cousin Teddy Roosevelt's footsteps.

discovered that Franklin had been having an affair with her social secretary, Lucy Mercer.

The Roosevelts' marriage had not been going well for some time. Franklin's mother had never warmed to her daughter-in-law and was a constant source of trouble and criticism. Both husband and wife were temperamentally unalike—he outgoing and cheerful, she reserved and lacking confidence—and slowly they had grown apart from each other, especially as Franklin's career had advanced. But Eleanor was distraught by the discovery of his unfaithfulness. She insisted that either the affair stop or she would demand a divorce, which in that period would have been a terrible social disgrace and meant the end of Franklin's political ambitions. He persuaded her that he would stop seeing Lucy Mercer, a promise he did not ultimately keep. After 1918, although they maintained a show of affection for the public's sake, Franklin and Eleanor Roosevelt were no longer in love. They did, however, develop a new working relationship with one another that was to prove enduring.

In 1920 Roosevelt ran as the Democratic vice presidential candidate for the White House alongside James Cox of Ohio. Unfortunately for both Roosevelt and Cox, the country was experiencing a backlash against the Woodrow Wilson years, and the Democratic platform, which included support for the new League of Nations—an early attempt at an organization like the United Nations—was unpopular. Franklin did not help matters by bragging (untruthfully)

> "The loneliest feeling in the world is when you think you are leading the parade and turn to find that no one is following you."
>
> —Quoted by Frances Perkins

at one point during the campaign that he had written the new constitution of Haiti while working for the navy. The Democrats were swept out of power by a large margin. Now out of a job, Roosevelt had to return to legal life in New York. This disappointment would pale, however, in comparison to the catastrophe that would befall him next.

One day in August 1921, while he was vacationing

on Campobello Island, Franklin grew strangely tired and felt one of his legs growing numb. "I tried to persuade myself that this trouble with my leg was muscular," he wrote later, "that it would disappear as I used it." But instead it grew worse, and soon he found he could not walk. Moreover, he was in great pain and running a high fever. The doctor eventually diagnosed the problem as infantile paralysis—now more commonly known as polio—a crippling and incurable disease that, as its name suggests, usually affected children. As he slowly recuperated under Eleanor's care, Franklin tried to put a brave face on this disaster: He wrote to his mother that "I have worn the braces hardly at all, I get lots of exercise crawling around, and I know the muscles are better than ever before. . . . I am in fine health and spend my time painting chairs, making boats and writing a history of the United States!" But Roosevelt's confidence was overly optimistic. He had been almost permanently paralyzed below the waist and could no longer move about without assistance. He would have to spend most of the rest of his life in a wheelchair.

For any 39-year-old man who enjoyed active hobbies like sports and sailing, this would have been terrible enough. But for a would-be presidential candidate like Roosevelt, the news was even more disastrous: Surely such a disability would make a future political career, with its strenuous campaigning and intense public scrutiny, next to impossible. From the start, Roosevelt was determined to prove this notion wrong. He spent

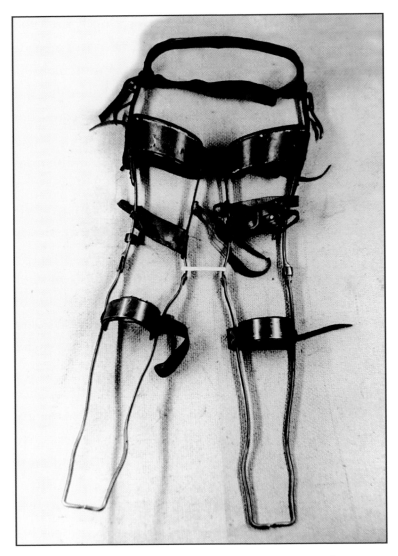

Roosevelt wore these heavy steel braces to help him regain some
of the mobility he lost when he became ill with the crippling
disease polio in 1921. Roosevelt spent the remainder of his life
using a wheelchair to get around; however, he managed to hide
the extent of his disability from the American public, avoiding
questions about his physical ability to perform the duties of
the president.

the next few years at expensive clinics and spas trying, without much success, to revive the use of his legs. But more important, he also began plotting a return to Democratic Party politics. He believed that the strength of his own willpower alone could overcome even this dreadful setback.

Roosevelt has been criticized by some for disguising the extent of his disability. He was careful never to be photographed in a wheelchair, and—amazingly, considering today's unsympathetic media standards—there was an unofficial agreement with the press and other political leaders not to portray him as paralyzed or to discuss his illness in public. Does this mean that Franklin was ashamed of his disability? Before judging too harshly, it is important to remember that in the 1920s and 1930s American society had different attitudes about the disabled than the ones held today. Someone who was "crippled" was generally considered too sickly or feeble to be able to lead a normal life, let alone hold high public office. Roosevelt had little choice but to mask the degree of his paralysis if he wished to pursue his political fortunes: It is unlikely that he could have ever secured the 1932 Democratic Party nomination, let alone win the presidential election, if he had openly campaigned in a wheelchair. Roosevelt never disguised the fact that he had suffered polio, and although ordinary Americans did not appreciate the extent to which this disease had disabled him, they did admire their president for his courage and determination in overcoming great pain and hardship.

Disability also changed Roosevelt personally. As a highly privileged young man, Franklin had sometimes acted haughtily, thoughtlessly, and even arrogantly toward other people: His selfish behavior toward Eleanor in the early years of their marriage was just one example. But his paralysis gave Franklin a new and unique insight into the experience of personal loss and suffering. He could never be so indifferent again to the difficulties that men and women of less fortunate backgrounds than his faced. His New Deal campaign in the 1930s was inspired by a deeply felt commitment to improving the lives of ordinary Americans who had also endured distress in the wake of the Great Depression.

While he tried to regain his health at Springwood—reading, writing, and working on his stamp collection (which eventually grew to well over a million stamps)—Roosevelt mulled over his return to public life. Politically speaking, his absence during most of the 1920s had its advantages, for these were bad years for the Democrats: Roosevelt was fortunate in being able to bide his time on the sidelines until his party's fortunes improved. In 1928, an opportunity beckoned. The Democratic presidential candidate that year, Al Smith, asked Roosevelt to run for the office of New York State governor. This, as Franklin had known all those years ago as a day-dreaming law clerk, was a natural springboard to the presidency; what's more, it had been Teddy's spring-board in 1900. But was the timing right? Was his health yet up to it? He agonized over the decision for weeks.

Roosevelt smiles as he receives news that he is winning the race for New York governor in 1928. His position as governor of New York State lay the political foundation for his run for the presidency in 1932, as it had done for his role model and cousin Teddy Roosevelt years earlier.

Finally, Roosevelt decided he could not pass up the offer. He agreed to run.

Despite the landslide victory of Republican Herbert Hoover in the presidential race that year, the Democratic Roosevelt scraped into the Governor's Mansion in New York by a thin margin of .6 percent. He had campaigned with astonishing vigor and speed, in part to dispel any concerns about his physical fitness for office, and he continued this energetic pace after the election. "Too bad about this unfortunate sick man, isn't it?" he once joked

Lincoln School Library

to reporters after recounting his strenuous work schedule. Roosevelt took his now deep-seated Progressive politics with him to Albany. Despite the opposition of a conservative Republican state legislature, Roosevelt introduced many ambitious government measures, including environmental laws, new safeguards for the elderly, electrification of upstate rural areas, and regulations on working conditions for women and minors. His popular activist measures, along with a mastery of the new publicity medium of radio that would become crucial during his later presidency, won Roosevelt statewide acclaim. He was reelected to a second term of office in 1930 by 750,000 votes, the largest margin in the history of New York.

By this time, however, a national emergency was brewing that would transform the politics of the next ten years. On October 26, 1929, share prices on the New York financial market slumped as a speculative stock bubble that had expanded out of proportion suddenly deflated—the infamous "Wall Street Crash." As the effects of the share collapse started to reverberate through the U.S. economy, companies and banks saw their profits dry up and commodity prices tumbled, putting farmers out of business. Within two years up to 14 million Americans were out of work; the "Great Depression," the worst economic crisis faced by the United States in the twentieth century, had begun. President Hoover, who had been an accomplished

> "Economic laws are not made by nature. They are made by human beings."
> —Roosevelt, speech, July 2, 1932

food-relief administrator during the World War I, was out of his depth. The cautious economic belief of the time was that politicians could do little to prevent depressions, and the only appropriate thing for the federal government to do was to *cut* budget spending rather than increase it—and certainly not to interfere with the workings of the free market, however bad things got. Hoover mostly accepted this traditional advice. The result was that the country sank deeper into depression.

Back in the New York governor's mansion, Roosevelt acted as far as he could to assist those people in his state affected by the ensuing economic collapse. In 1931, he created the first state agency in the United States to provide unemployment relief and fund new work for the jobless, the Temporary Emergency Relief Administration (TERA). This would be a model in miniature for many of the nationwide relief agencies set up in Roosevelt's presidency. He also badgered the legislature to introduce banking reforms and other proactive policies that might help poor and destitute New Yorkers. Roosevelt did not have an exact plan in mind as to how the government should reverse the crisis. Even after he became president, he introduced many different, and at times contradictory, measures: He did not bring a detailed philosophy of economic management to the White House. But Roosevelt had become convinced not only that the government *could* do more to help people suffering but also that it *must* do more; indeed, the federal government had a deep moral obligation to provide assistance to its

citizens. "Aid must be extended by government—
not as a matter of charity but as a matter of social
duty," he said in 1931. As the national crisis worsened,
Roosevelt became more and more certain that only he
could end the tragedy that was threatening to tear his
country apart.

Roosevelt's success in New York had made him a
natural Democratic candidate for the 1932 presidential
nomination. It was not a "shoe in," however: Al Smith,
who had talked Roosevelt into the governor's job back
in 1928, was running again, and Roosevelt's supporters
had to negotiate a difficult primary battle involving lots
of political negotiating among the different regional
factions of the Democratic party. When Roosevelt
finally clinched the nomination in July, he decided,
against tradition, to travel to the Chicago convention to
receive it directly. His acceptance speech was a master-
piece of political rhetoric, summarizing in a few
paragraphs the fears and hopes of millions of ordinary
Americans in a time of national emergency. Its most
famous passage is worth quoting in full:

> On the farms, in the large metropolitan areas, in
> the smaller cities and in the villages, millions of
> our citizens cherish the hope that their old
> standards of living and of thought have not gone
> forever. Those millions cannot and shall not hope
> in vain. I pledge you, I pledge myself, to a new deal
> for the American people. Let us all here assembled

constitute ourselves prophets of a new order of competence and of courage. This is more than a political campaign; it is a call to arms. Give me your help, not to win votes alone, but to win in this crusade to restore America to its own people.

Four months later, Franklin Delano Roosevelt defeated Herbert Hoover with 57.4 percent of the popular vote and became the 32nd President of the United States.

THE NEW DEAL:
1933–1940

UNDER THE CONSTITUTIONAL rules that still existed in 1932, a newly elected U.S. president did not officially take his oath of office in Washington, D.C., until the March after his victory—a gap of four months. This old tradition, which had worked well enough in the slower-paced world of Washington and Jefferson, was now dangerously out of date: The economic crisis was not prepared to wait out the winter until the new president took office. During January and February 1933, America sank into an even grimmer slump. Between one-quarter and one-third of the entire U.S. workforce was unemployed because of the collapse of businesses across the country. Hundreds of

Hoovervilles, towns of shacks and low-income housing, were a symptom of the harsh economic reality that had affected the country during President Herbert Hoover's administration. Many Americans could no longer afford to provide adequate shelter for their families and were instead forced to make do with the little resources that they had.

thousands of homeless and destitute people were living in makeshift refugee camps on the outskirts of big cities—known as Hoovervilles in a mocking tribute to the president. Up to 2 million more people were wandering the countryside, desperately looking for any kind of work that would help them feed their families. The American banking system was also on the brink of total failure, with 38 governors forced to close all the branches in their states to avoid financial panic. With the United

States effectively leaderless, the threat of mass riots, even political revolution, seemed close at hand.

Roosevelt, with his customary confidence, remained calm. Indeed, in the weeks leading up to his inauguration he seemed so unruffled that people began to accuse him of not taking the national crisis seriously enough. His decision to take a leisurely yacht cruise to the Bahamas in February seemed particularly insensitive, given the pain and anguish that millions of Americans were experiencing at that time. Actually, Roosevelt was hard at work during the trip developing his plans for the new presidency. When he returned to the mainland, he was involved in a private drama that put him in a different light. On the evening his yacht docked in Miami, Roosevelt made a speech to a small public audience. Afterward he chatted with his colleague and friend Anton Cermak, the mayor of Chicago, who happened to be visiting Florida at the time. The pair was talking in an open-topped car when suddenly a man jumped out of the crowd and fired a pistol at Roosevelt several times. All the bullets missed Roosevelt, but five other people were hit, including Mayor Cermak. As Secret Service agents grappled the would-be assassin to the ground, Roosevelt took control of the situation and calmly ordered his driver to take Cermak to the hospital. Cradling the dying man in his arms, Roosevelt remained composed throughout the whole ordeal and afterward shrugged off his brush with death as if it had never happened. His astonishing self-control in the face of personal danger won him many new admirers across the country. Later, this strength of will and cheerful optimism—even at the worst points of his presidency—would prove an inspiration to millions of Americans.

On March 4, 1933, Franklin Roosevelt gave his first inaugural address as president of the United States. Recognizing the tide of anxiety that was sweeping the nation, Roosevelt stressed the need for calm in midst of crisis: In words that were to become famous, he urged his countrymen to realize that "the only thing we have to fear is fear itself—nameless, unreasoning, unjustified terror which paralyzes needed efforts to convert retreat into advance." Once the

> "Let me assert my firm belief that the only thing we have to fear is fear itself."
> —Roosevelt, first Inaugural Address, March 4, 1933

formalities were over, Roosevelt quickly settled down to work. He began by ordering all the nation's banks to close for a few days, in a much-needed "holiday" to pacify panicking investors. Then he made the first of his special radio addresses to the American people, which were eventually known as Roosevelt's "Fireside Chats." These talks, which were written in an intimate, homey style, very different from the impersonal lectures that political leaders usually gave on the radio, were brilliant at creating the illusion that Roosevelt was speaking one-to-one with families across the country. His upbeat, self-assured manner was effective and helped renew popular confidence in the government. Once the banks reopened, people began to redeposit their savings. The immediate financial alarm was over, partly thanks to that well-timed Fireside Chat.

Roosevelt next ordered Congress to convene for a special emergency session. The first three months of this session, known as the "Hundred Days," saw a flurry of activity as new laws were hurriedly introduced to try to tackle the country's worst economic problems. Recalling Roosevelt's pledge at the Democratic Party convention the year before, the policies of the new administration were described as "The New Deal." Actually, when Roosevelt had used that phrase back in Chicago, he did not have a specific set of policies in mind. The New Deal was more of a random collection of ideas and initiatives than a carefully planned agenda. However, the expression captured the imaginations of Americans everywhere and became inseparable from Roosevelt's presidency: He would be known for the rest of his presidency as "Dr. New Deal."

> "We are trying to construct a more inclusive society. . . . We are going to make a country in which no one is left out."
>
> —Roosevelt's assessment of what the New Deal would achieve

An entire book could be dedicated to properly describing all of the events of the Hundred Days, which rank as one of the busiest and most productive periods in the history of the U.S. government. Ironically, one of Roosevelt's first actions was a painful flop. He introduced the

A common nickname for Roosevelt became "Dr. New Deal," a reference to the program of economic policies he implemented to heal the country's economic and political ills. This 1934 cartoon depicts "Dr. New Deal" Roosevelt with his bag of New Deal policies, ready to make changes in the country's "course of treatment" as needed.

Economy Act that drastically reduced payments to veterans and federal employees to skim $500 million off the budget. This was not only highly unpopular, it also made the economic situation even worse by lowering the amount of money available to consumers, stifling business growth. Cost cutting of this kind was at odds with many of Roosevelt's other New Deal schemes, and it just goes to show how little overall consistency there was behind many of his decisions. So far as the new president was concerned, the important thing was to act, and act quickly; the Depression could not wait for fine-tuned ideas. Roosevelt was unafraid to try new schemes, even those that were untested or contradictory. If they worked, he stuck by them; if they failed, he abandoned them. This willingness to challenge established notions came as a huge relief after Hoover's disastrous refusal to take any kind of risk at all, and even though some of Roosevelt's New Deal proposals were more successful than others, at least Americans felt reassured—at last, someone in Washington was doing *something* to help them.

Another of Roosevelt's early decisions was a lot more welcome than the Economy Act. For over a decade, "Prohibition" had made it illegal to sell alcohol in the United States, and apart from depriving people of a refreshing drink, it had encouraged widespread corruption and organized crime in America's big cities. In 1933, the 21st Amendment to the U.S. Constitution repealed Prohibition laws and allowed the consumption of beer and liquor once again. That same year another constitutional amendment, the 20th, changed the rules governing the timing of presidential terms. From now on, new presidents would enter office on the January 20 after their election. The dangerous four-month lapse that had almost wrecked the country in 1932 was gone at last.

The Hundred Days saw the creation of a series of federal laws and agencies intended to tackle various aspects of the Depression. These were jokingly referred to as "alphabet soup" because they were generally known by their three- or four-letter abbreviations. The first was the CCC (Civilian Conservation Corps), which recruited 120,000 jobless young men to work in the country's national parks and forests. The EFMA (Emergency Farm Mortgage Act) protected farmers from losing their homes and livelihoods if they could not pay their mortgages: Roosevelt later introduced a wider scheme for nonfarmers, known as the HOLC (Home Owners' Loan Corporation). One of the most ambitious new aid organizations was FERA (the Federal Emergency Relief Administration), run by Roosevelt's trusted adviser, Harry Hopkins. FERA was given $500 million by Congress to spend on welfare support for the unemployed and did much to help desperate citizens through the worst years of the Depression. The National Industrial Recovery Act, or NIRA, strengthened union rights and introduced government control of production and prices. Other early measures reorganized the nation's banks and stock markets to prevent the kind of near-catastrophes that had almost taken place in Hoover's presidency.

Unfortunately for Roosevelt, two of his biggest projects did not turn out so well. The NRA, or National Recovery Agency, was intended to draw up standard rules and practices for all American businesses, and to introduce agreements about minimum wages and maximum hours. In practice, the agency only managed to anger everyone—labor unions and businessmen alike—and failed in its bid to revive commercial trade. The AAA (Agricultural Adjustment Act) was a scheme to pay farmers to reduce their production, with the hope of raising agricultural prices: After some limited early success, this strategy failed to prove effective. The Supreme Court eventually decided that both the NRA and the AAA were unconstitutional and abolished them.

One of the best known of all Roosevelt's initiatives in the Hundred Days was the Tennessee Valley Authority, or TVA. In 1933, the area surrounding the Tennessee and Cumberland Rivers—including Tennessee itself, and also parts of Kentucky, Mississippi, Alabama, Georgia, and North Carolina—was among the poorest and least developed in the United States, and had been badly hit by the Great Depression. The TVA, a federally owned business, took over a large fertilizer manufacturer and hydroelectric plant at Muscle Shoals, Alabama, and began building a series of dams along the river systems to control their floodwaters and produce power. TVA initiatives introduced electricity to homes and farms across the region, replanted trees in deforested zones, fertilized the eroded soil, and cleaned up wildlife and fishing preserves. The TVA not only created many badly needed jobs and improved the quality of life for people across the southern United States, it was also one of the boldest environmental schemes that the federal government had attempted since FDR's cousin Teddy Roosevelt had created the Forest Service and expanded

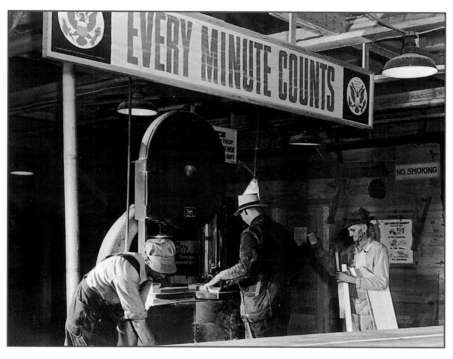

These laborers help construct the Douglas Dam on the French Broad River as part of Roosevelt's New Deal federal work program, the Tennessee Valley Authority (TVA). The TVA provided the unemployed with jobs and made physical improvements to the Tennessee Valley, helping to revive areas hit hard by the economic downturn of the 1930s.

the national park system 30 years earlier. The TVA is still in existence today, and is one of the many enduring legacies of the Hundred Days.

Perhaps Roosevelt's most urgent concern was to provide work for the jobless. He saw great evil in having so many millions of Americans unemployed, not only because of the hardship they were facing but also because their discontent might be harnessed by a would-be dictator. Roosevelt was well aware that just a few weeks before his inauguration, Adolf Hitler had come to power in Germany as "Fuehrer," or leader, partly through the support of angry unemployed workers. Roosevelt did not want the same fate for the United States. As he said in a Fireside Chat in 1938: "Not only our future economic soundness but the very soundness of our democratic institutions depends on the determination of our govern-ment to give employment to idle men." He had originally hoped that an agency called the PWA (Public Works Adminis-tration) would produce the necessary jobs, but its administrators took a timid approach to their mission and accomplished very little. Harry Hopkins, fresh from his success with the Federal Emergency Relief Administration, suggested a more ambitious job-creation scheme, which was to become the Civil Works Admin-istration, or CWA. At first, the CWA was a runaway success: In two months, Hopkins put 4 million Americans back to work in federal employment programs; however, Roosevelt was worried that the administration would grow so big that it would become a massive drain on the government's funds, so he closed it down. This was probably one of Roosevelt's biggest mistakes during his first term in office, because during its brief life the CWA not only created jobs but also gave a vital stimulus to the national economy. Roosevelt could be too cautious as well as too bold.

> *"People who are hungry and out of jobs are the stuff of which dictatorships are made."*
> —Roosevelt, State of the Union Address, 1944

The Hundred Days was a mixed bag of successes and failures. Although it did not completely turn back the Depression, at least it restored some badly needed confidence to the American people. A big part of that revival was simply due to Roosevelt's charismatic personality. Roosevelt was a master of public relations and knew exactly how to communicate his ideas to the public. He was an expert at using the press to advertise his policies and crafted his media image very carefully: It was not long before everyone in America instantly recognized his likeness, his trademark cigarette holder, and his toothy grin. Roosevelt inspired an extraordinary amount of affection within ordinary citizens, who came to see him not merely as a distant political leader but as a friend. He received 15 million letters from Americans during his presidency, a record still unmatched by any other resident of the White House. If Roosevelt was able to transform the mood of the country in the Hundred Days, it was not so much because of any specific policy he introduced but because he convinced people that there was someone in Washington who wanted to help them.

Eleanor's part in her husband's success should not be overlooked either. Ever since Franklin's incapacitation in 1921, she had taken over more and more public-speaking roles on his behalf, and she had become an accomplished political figure in her own right. Although their youthful love had never really rekindled after the Lucy Mercer affair, each of the Roosevelts respected and admired the other's abilities, and together they forged a unique

By making the press his ally, Roosevelt helped to influence the public's perception of him, his administration, and his policies. This alliance helped him win approval for many of his New Deal policies from both the public and Congress. His public image, which included his trademark cigarette holder and toothy grin, was that of a warm friend.

professional partnership. After Franklin's election, Eleanor became the most active First Lady in the country's history. She began weekly press conferences, presented her own radio show, wrote a widely syndicated newspaper column, and traveled across the United States lecturing and publicizing the ideas of the New Deal. She was particularly interested in the problems of women, the poor, and racial minorities, and was sometimes frustrated when she believed her husband's administration was not doing enough to help these groups. Eleanor was indispensable to Franklin in a way that no other presidential wife has ever been.

Despite his popularity, Roosevelt was certainly not short of critics on both the left and the right of politics. Influential businessmen distrusted Roosevelt because they believed he was undermining American capitalism and trying to introduce a kind of Russian-style state socialism. Some rich people particularly disliked him because they believed he was a traitor to his own social class. On the other hand, radicals complained that the New Deal had been too pro-business and had not really tried to alter the unequal distribution of wealth and power in the United States. Roosevelt was the kind of person whom people either adored or detested. It was difficult to have a neutral opinion about him. The rage that his name triggered in some people became a standing joke during his presidency: In one cartoon from *Esquire* magazine in 1938, an anxious child shouts to her mother that her brother "wrote a dirty word" on the sidewalk. The word turns out to be "Roosevelt"!

By 1935, the worst of the crisis that had faced America on Roosevelt's inauguration had passed, but the country's economy was still weak from the effects of the Depression. Roosevelt began a new round of initiatives, sometimes called the "Second New Deal." The most important of these were the WPA (Works Progress Administration), which spent more than $11 billion in job-creation funds over the next seven years; the NLRB (National Labor Relations Board), which guaranteed unions the right to

These women campaign to elect Roosevelt to a second presidential term in 1936. The empty basket of the woman on the right and the bountiful basket of the woman on the left illustrate the positive impact of Roosevelt's economic policies during his first term as president. Roosevelt easily won a second term.

bargain with management; and the social security system, which provided regular cash payments for the elderly, dependent children, and widows. These new programs were so popular that it is little wonder that Roosevelt won a smashing second victory in the 1936 presidential election, taking 46 of the 48 states that were then in the Union.

One interesting thing about Roosevelt's reelection was that it was the first time that many African-American voters had sided with the Democrats. Ever since the Civil War 70 years earlier, African-Americans had tended to

PRESIDENT ROOSEVELT'S LEGACY

Social Security

The first stage of the New Deal was concerned with tackling America's economic chaos in the midst of the Great Depression. Once the immediate crisis had receded, however, Roosevelt wanted to establish more long-term protection for the country's citizens, particularly the most vulnerable members of society, like the elderly. The Social Security Act, signed into law on August 14, 1935, was the keystone in his goal of a national welfare system. Under the act, workers paid a small percentage of their wages into a government fund (with employers also contributing) and in return they were guaranteed regular monthly benefits when they reached retirement age. The first payout—of 17 cents—was made to a man named Ernest Ackerman in January 1937.

In the more than six decades since Roosevelt's act, Social Security has become one of the most important practical legacies of the New Deal. Over 400 million Social Security numbers have been issued to Americans nationwide. The program—which was expanded in 1956 to include disability payments and in 1965 to include a form of health insurance called Medicare—has paid out nearly $6 trillion in benefits since its creation. In 1999, over 44 million retirees and other claimants were receiving Social Security each month, and the number is expected to increase. In fact, Social Security has been such a success that some people are concerned it will become too expensive to maintain in its present form. This will be one of the big welfare challenges of the twenty-first century.

remain loyal to Abraham Lincoln's Republican Party. In some ways, the switch was surprising, because the New Deal did not address the specific problems of race in America. Although Roosevelt occasionally talked about such issues—"No democracy can long survive which does not accept as fundamental to its very existence the recognition of the rights of minorities," he once wrote— he never spoke publicly about the racial injustice that was enforced by his own Democratic colleagues in the South. This was something that he was strongly criticized for at the time by civil rights supporters, including his own wife. But many poor African-Americans recognized that they benefited from the New Deal's programs, and they believed that, despite his blindness toward Jim Crow segregation, Roosevelt was still their natural ally.

Roosevelt's second term was not as successful as his first. He began by making a serious tactical mistake when he threatened to add six new members to the U.S. Supreme Court. Roosevelt had been angered by the court's destruction of the NRA and the AAA, and he believed that it unfairly favored big business over the New Deal. But although he described his proposal as a simple "reform" measure, Congress was horrified at the idea of the president trying to overturn the constitutional power of the legal branch, and Roosevelt was forced to abandon the idea. Also, the economic recovery that the country had begun to enjoy took a downturn in 1937, and this—combined with a series of industrial labor disputes—put increasing pressure on Roosevelt's administration. In the House and Senate elections of 1938, the Republicans won several seats, and Roosevelt was forced to scale back his plans for further recovery programs. Congress was becoming weary of Roosevelt's budgetary tinkering. The impetus of the New Deal slowly wound down during his second term in office.

Nonetheless, the crucial battle had been won. The country had been saved from economic chaos. Now, an even greater test would come to confront the Roosevelt presidency, this time from beyond America's borders.

5

THE
CHALLENGE
OF WAR:
1941–1945

IN THE SUMMER of 1940, the Democratic Party presidential convention in Chicago nominated Roosevelt for a third time. This was an unprecedented move. Ever since George Washington's decision to step down after his second term in office, no American president had ever served move than eight years in the White House. Although there was nothing in the Constitution that actually forbade Roosevelt from standing for president as many times as he wanted, to do so was a break in tradition that shocked many Americans. (The rules are now different: In 1951, Congress passed the 22nd Amendment to the Constitution, which prevents any candidate from serving more than two terms.)

Roosevelt, with Eleanor and vice president Henry Wallace and his wife, returns from his Hyde Park home after winning the 1940 election. Roosevelt remains the only U.S. president ever to have been elected for more than two terms. In 1951, Congress passed the 22nd Amendment to the Constitution, which limits presidents to serving only two terms.

Some of Roosevelt's political enemies suggested that he was power hungry and secretly wished to become a kind of elected dictator.

Actually, Roosevelt had been undecided about whether to run until late in 1940. Even Eleanor did not know what his final decision would be. On the one hand, he was not sure whether the American public would accept the same man as president three times running. On the other hand, however, he was concerned that the economy had not completely recovered from the Great Depression. Would a successor support the New Deal? And most important, Roosevelt was worried about the situation in Europe, where war had broken out the previous year. From 1940 onward, the emphasis in Roosevelt's presidency began to shift from domestic to international problems. The man who had spent his first two terms in the White House battling an economic crisis would now slowly transform into a war leader, defending American democracy from the tyranny of Nazi Germany and imperial Japan.

During the second half of the 1930s, the dictatorships of Europe and Asia—collectively known as the Axis powers—had begun aggressive campaigns of conquest. Germany, ruled by Fuehrer Adolf Hitler, had seized the countries of Austria, Czechoslovakia, and Poland. The attack on Poland in September 1939 provoked Great Britain and France to declare war, but the German army and air force were far better trained and equipped than those of their two enemies. In May 1940, the Nazis launched a devastating offensive against Western Europe, conquering France, Holland, Belgium, and much of Scandinavia in just a matter of weeks. Italy, ruled by the dictator Benito Mussolini, joined in the attack. Only the United Kingdom remained to fight the Axis, perilously defending itself from what looked like a coming German invasion. On the other side of the world, Japan's military rulers were involved in a brutal war against China, in which millions of soldiers and civilians were killed in terrible atrocities. To support their war effort, the Japanese were secretly considering another attack, this time on the oil and resource-rich territories of South East Asia such as Malaysia and Indonesia—and perhaps even the American-controlled Philippines. By 1940, the total victory of the Axis looked frighteningly close.

Roosevelt was alarmed by these overseas events and yearned to bring America into the fight against the Nazis and the Japanese militarists. He had no illusions about the danger that Hitler and the other dictators represented. As early as 1933, when the Fuehrer first became Chancellor of Germany, Roosevelt had said that "the man is a menace."

But even as powerful as Roosevelt was, he was still limited in what he could do to help other countries threatened by tyranny. In 1940, the American public was still strongly opposed to involvement in European or Asian politics. Five years earlier, Congress had passed the Neutrality Act, which made it illegal for Americans to sell or loan armaments to nations at war or lend them money. Roosevelt knew that if he tried to push for intervention abroad too quickly he would split the country and put his reelection into doubt, jeopardizing all the gains that the New Deal had made. He had no choice but to run as a peacemaker. "I have said this before, but I shall say it again and again and again," Roosevelt promised in a famous campaign speech, "your boys are not going to be sent into any foreign wars." Roosevelt won the 1940 election against his Republican

> *"When you see a rattlesnake poised to strike, you do not wait until he has struck to crush him."*
> —Roosevelt's explanation for his decision to seek out German submarines in the Atlantic Ocean

opponent Wendell Willkie by a comfortable margin, but his victory was due to the success of his economic reforms—definitely not because of his foreign policy.

Why were the American people so opposed to fighting the Axis at the beginning of World War II? It is important to remember that the United States had enjoyed a long and mostly peaceful isolation from the affairs of Europe and Asia, and there was a strong tradition of avoiding alliances with other countries—what George Washington had called dangerous "foreign entanglements." Many Americans believed that the British and French had tricked them into intervening in World War I, and they were determined not be dragged into far-off conflicts again. Furthermore, the United States had a small army at the beginning of the 1940s and it was not clear that a country only just recovering from economic chaos would be able to spend the enormous sums of money necessary to create a mighty military almost from scratch. It is worth keeping in mind that some of the worst crimes against humanity committed by the dictatorships, such as the mass killings of Jews by the Nazis, had not yet happened or been widely publicized. The German and Japanese governments had an ugly face, but few people really appreciated just how evil their policies would eventually become.

Despite his campaign pledges, Roosevelt believed that war against the Axis was inevitable, but he realized that he would have to persuade his fellow countrymen of this gradually. Roosevelt's immediate priority after the 1940 election was to try to give as much aid as possible to Great Britain, which was the only European country still fighting against the Nazis. The British had been able to thwart Hitler's attempt at invasion, but they were in a desperate position and rapidly running out of the money to buy new weapons. Roosevelt looked for ways to get around the restrictions of the Neutrality Act. He had already stumbled on one novel idea in August 1940 when he traded 50 old U.S. Navy destroyers to the British in return for leases on some of their worldwide naval bases. Now he proposed a much wider deal that he referred to as "Lend-Lease."

The Lend-Lease program, which would "loan" armaments to Britain without the need to pay for them, was not really the act of a neutral nation, but Roosevelt used his great powers of public speaking to convince the American people that Lend-Lease was just a sensible defensive precaution. "There is far less chance of the United States getting into war if we do all we can now to support the nations defending themselves against attack by the Axis than if we acquiesce [accept] in their defeat," he said. Roosevelt spoke of the United States as the "great arsenal of democ-

> "We have the men—the skill—the wealth—and above all, the will. . . . We must be the great arsenal of democracy."
> —Roosevelt, Fireside Chat, December 29, 1940

racy." At the same time he was helping Great Britain, Roosevelt also ordered a large increase in spending on the U.S. military, and he introduced the Selective Service Act, the country's first peacetime draft.

These warplanes were given to Britain as part of Roosevelt's Lend-Lease policy before the United States entered World War II. The Lend-Lease Act allowed Britain easier access to weaponry to defend itself against the Axis countries. Warships, tanks, and artillery were also part of the deal.

Throughout 1941, the United States edged closer toward confrontation with the Axis powers, particularly Nazi Germany. At the beginning of the year, Roosevelt made a major speech in which he talked about the "Four Freedoms" essential for a future world of peace and prosperity. These liberties—freedom of expression, freedom of religious worship, freedom from want, and freedom from fear—would be the basis of his support for the countries fighting against Germany and Japan. Inspiring ideas such as the Four Freedoms did much to persuade ordinary Americans of the importance of defending democracy abroad. At this time Roosevelt also began a close partnership with the British prime minister Winston Churchill, who was eager to get the United States into the war as soon as possible. The two met onboard ship at Placentia Bay, Newfoundland, in August 1941, and in addition to making some important practical decisions about British-American military cooperation, Roosevelt and Churchill also announced the Atlantic Charter, a set of general principles shared by both their countries—including an open call for "the destruction of the Nazi tyranny."

During the summer and fall of 1941, American eyes were glued on the deadly battle in the North Atlantic. German submarines, or U-boats, were trying to sink as many British merchant ships as possible, preventing the transport of supplies and food to the United Kingdom and so starving Great Britain into submission. Roosevelt wanted the United States to intervene in the Battle of the Atlantic, partly to help the British, but also because it would be the perfect opportunity to create an "incident" with Germany that might provoke outright war. He did not have long to wait. In June, the first American freighter was sunk; in September, a German U-boat unsuccessfully attacked a U.S. Navy destroyer; in mid-October, another destroyer was hit and damaged by a German torpedo. Finally, on October 31, the USS *Reuben James* was sunk with 115 men killed, the first American warship lost in World War II. Roosevelt used each incident to peel away sections of the Neutrality Act and increase military support for Britain. However, by the beginning of December 1941, the United States and Germany still remained technically, though precariously, at peace.

When war finally came to America, it arrived from a totally unexpected direction. Although most attention had been fixed on events in the Atlantic, drama was also stirring in the Pacific. Relations between the United States and Japan had been deteriorating throughout 1941. In July, the United States placed an embargo on all oil shipments to Japan, which would make it impossible for the military leaders in Tokyo to continue their war against China. The Japanese had to either abandon their territorial goals or seize the British and Dutch oil wells in Southeast Asia, which would mean war with America. They chose to fight. Intelligence agents in Washington had broken the Japanese radio codes, so they had some idea that conflict was brewing, but they assumed that any war would begin with an attack on the Philippines. The Japanese military had a more ambitious plan.

On December 7, 1941, thousands of lives were lost as the Japanese attacked Pearl Harbor, thus drawing the United States into World War II. With Great Britain and the Soviet Union as its allies, the United States was now in a position take on the Axis countries.

On the morning of Sunday, December 7, 1941 — "a date which will live in infamy," as Roosevelt called it in his address to Congress the following day — Japanese aircraft attacked the unsuspecting U.S. Navy base at Pearl Harbor in Hawaii. Five battleships were sunk and more than 2,300 American servicemen were killed. On December 11, Germany also declared war on the United States. The Axis countries were now

> "Yesterday, December 7, 1941 — a date which will live in infamy — the United States of America was suddenly and deliberately attacked by naval and air forces of the Empire of Japan."
>
> —Roosevelt, Address to Congress declaring war on Japan, December 8, 1941

confronted by the Allied powers of the United States, Great Britain, and the Soviet Union (which Germany had attacked in June 1941) in a struggle for nothing less than the mastery of the planet.

Roosevelt's main role for the next 40 months was as commander in chief of the U.S. armed forces. It is interesting to compare the way that Roosevelt led his country's military with the style of his fellow world leaders. Hitler and the Russian dictator Josef Stalin often interfered with their generals' decisions, overruling them on small points of detail and generally obstructing the efficient running of the war. Even Winston Churchill tended to meddle too much in technical affairs that he did not really understand, although fortunately his military advisors were able to talk him out of some of his wilder schemes. Roosevelt, by contrast, had the wisdom to respect the professional advice of his senior commanders. He was particularly lucky that his chief of staff, General George C. Marshall, was one of the most talented administrators ever produced by the U.S. Army: when Marshall was proposed as the leader of the D day invasion of France, Roosevelt overruled the decision, saying that he could not sleep peacefully at night unless he knew Marshall was in Washington, D.C.

Leaving the day-to-day decision making to Marshall and his staff, Roosevelt devoted his time to tackling the larger strategic problems of the war and issues affecting the home front. He spent much of his time at the Hyde Park estate, working on documents or meeting important guests such as Churchill. Because there was too much noise at Springwood, Roosevelt had a private retreat built a few miles away from the main house, a little bungalow called Top Cottage that was secluded enough to give him some valuable privacy. His devoted companion at Top Cottage was Fala, a black Scottish terrier who was given to the president in 1940 and who became, along with the cigarette holder, one of Roosevelt's most easily recognized trademarks. In quieter moments away from the tensions of war Roosevelt also enjoyed planting trees on the estate, particularly his favorite, the tulip poplar: Roosevelt always described himself as a "tree farmer" above all things.

Much of Roosevelt's time was spent dealing with wartime domestic concerns. The surprise Japanese attack had united the American people in a determination to defeat the Axis powers, and even businessmen who had been suspicious of the New Deal were willing to cooperate with Roosevelt's new programs, such as the War Production Board (WPB) and the Office of War Mobilization (OWM), so long as it meant supporting the fighting effort. America's civilian industries were quickly transformed into the "great arsenal of democracy" Roosevelt had proclaimed in 1940. However, great controversies were still apparent on the home front. Business leaders criticized the government for causing bureaucratic confusion. There were complaints about rationing and price controls. Labor disputes with the coal miner's union became so fierce that in 1943, responding to a strike, Roosevelt seized the mines and forced the miners back into production at bayonet-point.

Roosevelt also proved he could be ruthless in matters of race. In the immediate aftermath of the Pearl Harbor attack, suspicion and anger had fallen on the tens of thousands of Japanese-American people living in the United States, particularly in California and on the West Coast. Although there was little evidence that these families—many of which had lived in America for generations—posed any real security threat to the country, claims of disloyalty and allegations of spying and sabotage surrounded them. In February 1942, in one of his most notorious decisions, Roosevelt issued an executive order allowing the authorities to forcibly expel certain people from coastal areas according to their racial origin. Around 112,000 Japanese-Americans, two-thirds of them U.S. citizens, were moved to internment centers elsewhere in the country. Eleanor, who had a strong interest in civil rights issues, was particularly shocked by the decision, but could do nothing. In 1944, Roosevelt refused to repeal the order even when he was advised that it was no longer militarily necessary. Although Roosevelt probably acted more for political reasons than any genuine distrust of Japanese-Americans, the internment was one of the low points of his presidency. In 1988, surviving internees were awarded compensation for their ordeal, and five years later President Clinton made a formal apology on behalf of the U.S. government.

Roosevelt's international decisions were more admirable. He attended a series of important conferences with the other Allied leaders, in part to coordinate the military campaign against the Axis, but also to negotiate the organization of the postwar world. In January 1943, he traveled to Casablanca in Morocco to meet with Churchill and begin the planning of the D day offensive, which took place 17 months later, in June 1944. At Casablanca, Roosevelt announced, possibly as an off-the-cuff remark, that the Allies would demand nothing less than "unconditional surrender" by Germany, Italy, and Japan—in other words, there would be no negotiations. Although some people later criticized this announcement, saying that it prolonged the war, Roosevelt was probably right that it was the only way to make sure all Axis countries were permanently rid of Nazism and militarism. In November 1943, he and Churchill met with Stalin together for the first time in Tehran, Iran. The atmosphere between the two Western leaders and the Communist dictator was frosty, but Roosevelt hoped that they had laid the groundwork for cooperation after the war.

In 1944, Roosevelt was due for reelection for an unprecedented fourth term as U.S. president. This no longer shocked people: Indeed, Roosevelt had been in the White House for so long that it was becoming hard to imagine the presidency without him. The war was going well and looked as if it would soon be over, and about 70 percent of voters approved of Roosevelt's policies at home and abroad. The main difficulty, which the Washington administration tried its best to hide, was Roosevelt's failing health. The toll of 12 strenuous years in office was at last beginning to affect him. To deflect suspicion that he was seriously ill, Roosevelt did a number of stunts such as driving for four hours in the pouring rain in an open-topped campaign procession through New York City. His stamina was visibly flagging, however. He won the election without much difficulty, but he was finding it harder and harder to work for long periods. In truth, Roosevelt was slowly dying.

Roosevelt made one more major international appearance at the Russian Black Sea resort of Yalta in February 1945 where, along with Churchill and Stalin, he drew up plans for the postwar division of Europe between East and West. The agreement at Yalta meant leaving millions of eastern Europeans within the Communist sphere—behind the Iron Curtain, as Churchill later put it—but with Russia's Red Army now in effective control of much of this territory anyway, there did not seem to be much either the Americans or the British could do about it. The plan was not idealistic, but at least it was practical and would ensure some kind of permanent peace settlement after years of devastating warfare. At the Yalta meeting Churchill, Stalin, and Roosevelt also discussed the future United Nations Organization, which was intended to be a more effective replacement for the old League of Nations. Roosevelt was determined that the United States would never again lapse into the kind of diplomatic isolationism he had battled before Pearl Harbor. "Responsibility for political conditions thousands of miles away can no longer be avoided, I think, by this great Nation," he said in an address to Congress on March 1, 1945.

Churchill, Roosevelt, and Stalin gathered at the Yalta Conference to determine how Europe was to be reorganized after World War II and what was to be done with those countries conquered or destroyed by Germany. The three leaders also discussed the future United Nations Organization.

One thing Roosevelt did not reveal to Stalin at Yalta was that scientists working in New Mexico were close to completing a new weapon with an incredible destructive power: the atomic bomb, or A-bomb. This was such a closely guarded secret that even the man who would eventually order the dropping of the two A-bombs on Japan, Roosevelt's vice president Harry Truman, did not know about their existence yet.

During the weeks that followed Yalta, Roosevelt's strength deteriorated even more rapidly. His friends and colleagues were shocked at his gray, ashen appearance: "When he was wheeled in I was so startled I almost burst into tears," said his personal secretary Grace Tully. To try to recuperate his health, Roosevelt decided to visit his family's vacation home in Warm Springs, Georgia. Eleanor did not accompany him, but Lucy Mercer—the woman with whom he had had an affair almost 30 years earlier—

PRESIDENT ROOSEVELT'S LEGACY

The United Nations

On January 1, 1942, less than a month after the attack on Pearl Harbor, representatives of Great Britain, the USSR, China, and more than 20 other countries met in Washington, D.C., to sign an agreement committing themselves to victory against the Axis powers of Germany, Italy, and Japan. On Roosevelt's suggestion, this was called "the Declaration by United Nations," and the name invented by the president stuck. The Allies were officially known from then on as the "United Nations," or the UN.

The military defeat of the Axis took precedence over other matters during the next three years, but as the end of the Second World War grew closer, the idea of turning the United Nations into a permanent body dedicated to international peace and security found more and more supporters. At the Tehran Conference in December 1943, Roosevelt, Churchill, and Stalin agreed in principle to the founding of a postwar UN organization, and during the following year, its future structure and rules were thrashed out at meetings of the big Allied powers. On April 25, 1945— just 13 days after Roosevelt's death—delegates of 50 nations met in San Francisco to draw up the Charter of the United Nations. This was finally ratified by the major Allied governments on October 24 that year, which is considered the birthday of the UN. Although Roosevelt did not live to take part in the organization he named and worked so hard to create, Eleanor Roosevelt was an important member of the UN for many years and helped draft its Declaration of Human Rights.

did. Lucy had been married and widowed, and during the war years she and Roosevelt had secretly begun to meet again. At Warm Springs, Roosevelt seemed at first to revive his spirits. Then, on Thursday afternoon, April 12, 1945, Roosevelt was sitting for a watercolor portrait when he began complaining of a severe headache. Suddenly, he slumped forward in his wheelchair, unconscious. The doctor was called, but nothing could be done. Franklin Delano Roosevelt, the longest-serving president in U.S. history, died of a brain hemorrhage. He was 63 years old.

6

AMERICA TRANSFORMED

THE ANNOUNCEMENT THAT Roosevelt was dead came as a great shock to the American people. Many of them had seen from the movie newsreels just how frail and ill their president had become by the beginning of 1945, but still it seemed difficult to imagine a United States without him. He had dominated the country's public life for more than 13 years and had come to symbolize for millions the hopes

> "I do not look upon these United States as a finished product. We are still in the making."
>
> —Roosevelt's words on the progress of the United States

and aspirations of a better America. "What can we say? What can we do?" wrote an Atlanta newspaper. On hearing the news, some people wept openly in the streets. It seemed particularly cruel that Roosevelt should be struck down just as the victory of the Allied armies against Germany and Japan drew close.

Eleanor was in Washington, D.C., attending a concert on April 12. She had received a phone call from Georgia earlier in the day, but was told only that the president had fainted, so she did not realize the seriousness of the situation. As the concert continued, an urgent call came from the White House asking her to return. Sensing that something was very wrong, Eleanor rushed back to Pennsylvania Avenue. There, Roosevelt's weeping press secretary told her that her husband was dead. With great composure and bravery, similar to that which Roosevelt had displayed when Anton Cermak was killed in 1933, Eleanor asked for the vice president, Harry Truman, to be summoned. When Truman arrived, she placed an arm on his shoulder and said softly, "Harry, the president is dead." The astonished Truman asked if there was anything he could do for her. Eleanor replied, "Is there anything we can do for you? You are the one in trouble now."

The following day, Roosevelt's coffin, draped in an American flag, was slowly carried by presidential train from Georgia northward to Washington. Thousands of ordinary people lined the route to pay their respects to

On August 19, 1945, four months after his death, Americans remembered the life of Roosevelt on what President Harry S. Truman proclaimed as a day of prayer. Here, Eleanor Roosevelt broadcasts a message of comfort about her husband's death to the people of the United States.

a man they had never met, but with whom they felt they shared a long personal friendship. After lying in state at the White House with full military honors, Roosevelt was escorted by a small guard of cadets to Hyde Park, where on the morning of April 15 he was buried in the Rose Garden at his beloved Springwood estate. Some 17 years later, after a distinguished career as a stateswoman and writer, Eleanor Roosevelt joined her husband at the Rose Garden burial site. Also buried nearby was Roosevelt's famous little dog Fala and another dog owned by Franklin and Eleanor's daughter Anna.

The author John Gunther wrote in 1950 that "the President, though dead, is still alive. Millions of Americans will continue to vote for Roosevelt as long as they live." The work that Roosevelt began during his lifetime endured long after his passing. Harry Truman, who succeeded Roosevelt as the 33rd president of the United States, concluded the victorious war against Germany in May 1945 and against Japan three months later. That October, the United Nations Organization was officially founded, the product of Roosevelt's long negotiations with Churchill and Stalin. In the United States itself, the government agencies, either directly created or inspired by the New Deal, permanently changed the lives of generations of

> *"In our seeking for economic and political progress as a nation, we all go up—or else all go down—as one people."*
> —Roosevelt, Inaugural Address, March 4, 1937

Roosevelt's flag-draped casket moves toward the final resting place of the president at his family estate in Hyde Park on April 15, 1945. In his more than 12 years as president of the United States, Roosevelt instilled a sense of optimism and a confirmed belief in the virtues of democracy in the American people.

Americans. Perhaps Roosevelt's greatest legacy to his countrymen and-women was, however, his unbounded optimism throughout times of hardship, private as well as public. In 1933, Roosevelt had assumed leadership of a nation in despair: He bequeathed to his successors a prosperous land, full of hope and confirmed in its belief in the basic principles of American democracy. For that achievement alone, historians and scholars consider Franklin Delano Roosevelt the greatest American president of the twentieth century.

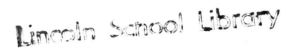

THE PRESIDENTS
OF THE
UNITED STATES

George Washington
1789–1797

John Adams
1797–1801

Thomas Jefferson
1801–1809

James Madison
1809–1817

James Monroe
1817–1825

John Quincy Adams
1825–1829

Andrew Jackson
1829–1837

Martin Van Buren
1837–1841

William Henry
Harrison
1841

John Tyler
1841–1845

James Polk
1845–1849

Zachary Taylor
1849–1850

Millard Filmore
1850–1853

Franklin Pierce
1853–1857

James Buchanan
1857–1861

Abraham Lincoln
1861–1865

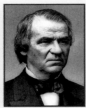

Andrew Johnson
1865–1869

Ulysses S. Grant
1869–1877

Rutherford B. Hayes
1877–1881

James Garfield
1881

Chester Arthur
1881–1885

Grover Cleveland
1885–1889

Benjamin Harrison
1889–1893

Grover Cleveland
1893-1897

William McKinley
1897–1901

Theodore Roosevelt
1901–1909

William H. Taft
1909–1913

Woodrow Wilson
1913–1921

Warren Harding
1921–1923

Calvin Coolidge
1923–1929

Herbert Hoover
1929–1933

Franklin D. Roo-
sevelt 1933–1945

Harry S. Truman
1945–1953

Dwight Eisenhower
1953–1961

John F. Kennedy
1961–1963

Lyndon Johnson
1963–1969

Richard Nixon
1969–1974

Gerald Ford
1974–1977

Jimmy Carter
1977–1981

Ronald Reagan
1981–1989

George H.W. Bush
1989–1993

William J. Clinton
1993–2001

George W. Bush
2001–

Note: Dates indicate years of
presidential service.
Source: www.whitehouse.gov

PRESIDENTIAL FACT FILE

THE CONSTITUTION

Article II of the Constitution of the United States outlines several requirements for the president of the United States, including:

- ★ **Age:** The president must be at least 35 years old.
- ★ **Citizenship:** The president must be a U.S. citizen.
- ★ **Residency:** The president must have lived in the United States for at least 14 years.
- ★ **Oath of Office:** On his inauguration, the president takes this oath: "I do solemnly swear (or affirm) that I will faithfully execute the office of President of the United States, and will to the best of my ability, preserve, protect and defend the Constitution of the United States."
- ★ **Term:** A presidential term lasts four years.

PRESIDENTIAL POWERS

The president has many distinct powers as outlined in and interpreted from the Constitution. The president:

- ★ Submits many proposals to Congress for regulatory, social, and economic reforms.
- ★ Appoints federal judges with the Senate's approval.
- ★ Prepares treaties with foreign nations to be approved by the Senate.
- ★ Can veto laws passed by Congress.
- ★ Acts as commander in chief of the military to oversee military strategy and actions.
- ★ Appoints members of the Cabinet and many other agencies and administrations with the Senate's approval.
- ★ Can declare martial law (control of local governments within the country) in times of national crisis.

PRESIDENTIAL FACT FILE

TRADITION

Many parts of the presidency developed out of tradition. The traditions listed below are but a few that are associated with the U.S. presidency.

- ★ After taking his oath of office, George Washington added, "So help me God." Numerous presidents since Washington have also added this phrase to their oath.

- ★ Originally, the Constitution limited the term of the presidency to four years, but did not limit the number of terms a president could serve. Presidents, following the precedent set by George Washington, traditionally served only two terms. After Franklin Roosevelt was elected to four terms, however, Congress amended the Constitution to restrict presidents to only two.

- ★ James Monroe was the first president to have his inauguration outside the Capitol. From his inauguration in 1817 to Jimmy Carter's inauguration in 1977, it was held on the Capitol's east portico. Ronald Reagan broke from this tradition in 1981 when he was inaugurated on the west portico to face his home state, California. Since 1981, all presidential inaugurations have been held on the west portico of the Capitol.

- ★ Not all presidential traditions are serious, however. One of the more fun activities connected with the presidency began when President William Howard Taft ceremoniously threw out the first pitch of the new baseball season in 1910.  Presidents since Taft have carried on this tradition, including Woodrow Wilson, who is pictured here as he throws the first pitch of the 1916 season. In more recent years, the president has also opened the All-Star and World Series games.

PRESIDENTIAL FACT FILE

THE WHITE HOUSE

Although George Washington was involved with the planning of the White House, he never lived there. It has been, however, the official residence of every president beginning with John Adams, the second U.S. president. The  building was completed approximately in 1800, although it has undergone several renovations since then. It was the first public building constructed in Washington, D.C. The White House has 132 rooms, several of which are open to the public. Private rooms include those for administration and the president's personal residence. For an online tour of the White House and other interesting facts, visit the official White House website, *http://www.whitehouse.gov.*

THE PRESIDENTIAL SEAL

A committee began planning the presidential seal in 1777. It was completed in 1782. The seal appears as an official stamp on medals, stationery, and documents, among other items. Originally, the eagle faced right toward the arrows (a symbol of war) that it held in its talons. In 1945, President Truman had the seal altered so that the eagle's head instead faced left toward the olive branch (a symbol of peace), because he believed the president should be prepared for war but always look toward peace.

PRESIDENT ROOSEVELT IN PROFILE

PERSONAL

Name: Franklin Delano Roosevelt

Birth date: January 30, 1882

Birth place: Hyde Park, New York

Father: James Roosevelt

Mother: Sara Delano

Wife: Anna Eleanor Roosevelt

Children: Anna Eleanor, James, Elliott, Franklin Delano, Jr., John Aspinwall

Death date: April 12, 1945

Death place: Warm Springs, Georgia

POLITICAL

Years in office: 1933–1945

Vice president: John N. Garner (1933–41); Henry A. Wallace (1941–45); Harry S. Truman (1945)

Occupations before presidency: Lawyer, member of the New York State legislature, assistant secretary of the U.S. Navy, governor of New York

Political party: Democrat

Major achievements of presidency:
New Deal policies instituted to stabilize economy during the Great Depression, World War II, laid groundwork for United Nations, rebuilt American faith in democracy

Nickname: Dr. New Deal, FDR

Presidential library:

Franklin D. Roosevelt Presidential Library
4079 Albany Post Road
Hyde Park, NY 12538
(800) FDR-VISIT
http://www.fdrlibrary.marist.edu

Tributes:

Home of Franklin D. Roosevelt
(Hyde Park, NY; *http://www.nps.gov/hofr/*);

Franklin Delano Roosevelt Memorial
(Washington, D.C.; *http:www.nps.gov/fdrm/home.htm*);

FDR's Little White House
(Warm Springs, GA; *http://www.fdr-littlewhitehouse.org/*)

CHRONOLOGY

1882   Franklin Delano Roosevelt is born at Springwood, Hyde Park, New York.

1896–1900   Roosevelt attends Groton School.

1900–1904   Roosevelt attends Harvard University, where he meets Anna Eleanor Roosevelt.

1901–1908   Franklin's cousin Theodore ("Teddy") Roosevelt serves as president of the United States.

1904–1910   Roosevelt attends Columbia Law School, takes the New York bar examination and becomes a Manhattan law clerk.

1905   Franklin and Eleanor are married.

1910   Roosevelt is elected to the New York State Senate. He is reelected in 1912.

1913–1920   Serves as assistant secretary of the navy in President Woodrow Wilson's administration.

1917–1918   The United States intervenes in World War I.

1920   Roosevelt is defeated in his run for the vice presidency.

1921   Roosevelt contracts polio while staying on Campobello Island and is paralyzed mostly from the waist down. Spends most of the next seven years recuperating.

1928   Roosevelt is elected Governor of New York. He is reelected in 1930.

1929   The Wall Street Crash heralds the beginning of the Great Depression.

1932   Nominated as Democratic party candidate for the presidency, Roosevelt makes his famous "New Deal" pledge. Roosevelt is elected president, defeating the incumbent Herbert Hoover.

1933 Unsuccessful assassination attempted on Roosevelt in Florida. He begins the New Deal with his "Hundred Days" of rapid legislation. Prohibition is repealed.

1935 Roosevelt introduces the "Second New Deal," including the Social Security program. The Neutrality Act is passed.

1936 Roosevelt is re-elected president.

1937 He fails in his attempt to add extra judges to the Supreme Court. Two-year economic recession begins. Japan invades China.

1939 World War II begins in Europe when Great Britain and France declare war on Germany after it invades Poland.

1940 Roosevelt is reelected president, becoming the first man ever to hold the office more than twice. Germany conquers most of Western Europe.

1941 Roosevelt makes "Four Freedoms" speech. Lend-Lease to Great Britain is introduced. Roosevelt and Winston Churchill meet at Placentia Bay and Roosevelt announces "Atlantic Charter." Confrontation occurs between German U-boats and U.S. Navy ships in Atlantic. Japan attacks U.S. Pacific Fleet at Pearl Harbor, bringing the United States into World War II.

1942 The internment of Japanese-Americans begins. The "Declaration of United Nations" is announced.

1943 Roosevelt meets with Churchill at Casablanca, Morocco, to plan D day invasion. Later, the two also meet with Stalin in Tehran, Iran.

1944 Allies perform D day invasion of Europe. Roosevelt is reelected president for fourth term.

1945 Roosevelt, Churchill and Stalin meet at Yalta, USSR, to plan United Nations and the postwar division of Europe. Roosevelt dies in Warm Springs, Georgia.

BIBLIOGRAPHY

Buhite, Russell D., and Levy, David W., eds. *FDR's Fireside Chats.* Norman, OK: University of Oklahoma, 1992.

Maney, Patrick. *The Roosevelt Presence.* New York: Simon & Schuster, 1992.

McElvaine, Robert. *Franklin Delano Roosevelt.* Washington, D.C.: CQ Press, 2002.

Ward, Geoffrey. *Before the Trumpet: Young Franklin Roosevelt, 1882–1905.* New York: Harper & Rowe, 1985.

Whitney, Sharon. *Eleanor Roosevelt.* New York: Franklin Watts, 1982.

Freedman, Russell. *Franklin Delano Roosevelt*. Boston: Houghton Mifflin Company, 1992.

Friedel, Frank. *Franklin D. Roosevelt: A Rendezvous with Destiny*. New York: Little Brown & Company, 1991.

Goodwin, Doris Kearns. *No Ordinary Time: Franklin and Eleanor Roosevelt—The Home Front in World War II*. New York: Simon & Schuster, 1994.

Grapes, Bryan J. *Franklin D. Roosevelt*. Detroit: Gale Group, 2000.

Roosevelt, Franklin. *Great Speeches: Franklin Delano Roosevelt*. John Grafton, ed. New York: Dover Publications, 1999.

Winthrop, Elizabeth. *Dear Mr. President: Franklin Delano Roosevelt: Letters from a Mill Town Girl*. New York: Winslow Press, 2001.

FURTHER READING

WEBSITES

The Age of Franklin D. Roosevelt, 1933–1945
http://ericir.syr.edu/Virtual/Lessons/crossroads/sec2/essay10.html

America in the 1930s
http://xroads.virginia.edu/~1930s/front.html

The American Experience: The President
http://www.pbs.org/wgbh/amex/presidents/

The American Presidency
www.grolier.com/presidents/

American President
http://www.americanpresident.org

FDR Cartoon Archive
http://www.nisk.k12.ny.us/fdr/

Fireside Chats of Franklin D. Roosevelt
http://www.mhric.org/fdr/fdr.html

Franklin and Eleanor Roosevelt Institute
http://www.feri.org/

Franklin D. Roosevelt Presidential Library and Museum
http://www.fdrlibrary.marist.edu

Franklin Delano Roosevelt Memorial Park
http://www.nps.gov/fdrm/

The New Deal Network
http://newdeal.feri.org/

Voices of World War II: Experiences from the Front and at Home
http://www.umkc.edu/lib/spec-col/ww2/

"We Made Do": Recalling the Great Depression
http://www.mcsc.k12.in.us/mhs/social/madedo/

The White House: Franklin Delano Roosevelt
http://www.whitehouse.gov/history/presidents/fr32.html

INDEX

INDEX

PICTURE CREDITS

page:

11: © Bettmann/CORBIS
15: Courtesy of the FDR Library
18: Courtesy of the FDR Library
21: Courtesy of the FDR Library
26: © Hulton|Archive, by Getty Images
29: Courtesy of the FDR Library
32: Courtesy of the FDR Library
35: © Hulton|Archive, by Getty Images
41: © Hulton|Archive, by Getty Images
45: Courtesy of the Library of Congress,
    LC-USZ62-17305

49: Courtesy of the FDR Library
52: Courtesy of the FDR Library
54: Public Domain
59: Courtesy of the FDR Library
64: Courtesy of the FDR Library
67: Courtesy of the FDR Library
73: © Hulton-Deutsch Collection/
    CORBIS
78: © Associated Press, AP
80: © Associated Press, AP

Cover: © Oscar White/CORBIS

ACKNOWLEDGMENTS

Thank you to Celebrity Speakers Intl. for coordinating Mr. Cronkite's contribution to this book.

ABOUT THE CONTRIBUTORS

Alan Allport was born in Whiston, England, and grew up in East Yorkshire. He has a master's degree in history from the University of Pennsylvania and is currently a Ph.D. candidate at that institution, with a special interest in nineteenth- and twentieth-century European history. He is currently working on projects connected to the social and cultural histories of the two world wars. He lives in Philadelphia.

Walter Cronkite has covered virtually every major news event during his more than 60 years in journalism, during which he earned a reputation for being "the most trusted man in America." He began his career as a reporter for the United Press during World War II, taking part in the beachhead assaults of Normandy and covering the Nuremberg trials. He then joined *CBS News* in Washington, D.C., where he was the news anchor for political convention and election coverage from 1952 to 1980. CBS debuted its first half-hour weeknight news program with Mr. Cronkite's interview of President John F. Kennedy in 1963. Mr. Cronkite was inducted into the Academy of Television Arts and Sciences in 1985 and has written several books. He lives in New York City with his wife of 59 years.